THE TEMPEST

ILLUSTRATED BY
PAUL DUFFIELD

SELF
MADE
HERO

SELF MADE HERO

Published by
SelfMadeHero
A division of Metro Media Ltd
5 Upper Wimpole Street
London W1G 6BP
www.selfmadehero.com

This edition published 2007

Illustrator: Paul Duffield
Text Adaptor: Richard Appignanesi
Designer: Andy Huckle
Textual Consultant: Nick de Somogyi
Publisher: Emma Hayley

ISBN-13: 978-0-9552856-2-2

10 9 8 7 6 5 4 3 2
Printed and bound in China

Prospero, wizard and real Duke of Milan

"We are such stuff as dreams are made on…"

Miranda, daughter of Prospero

"O brave new world that has such people in it!"

Ferdinand, son of King Alonso

"I'll make you the Queen of Naples."

Caliban, a witch's son and Prospero's slave

"Freedom, high-day, high-day freedom!"

"Remember I have done thee worthy service."

Ariel, Prospero's spirit-servant

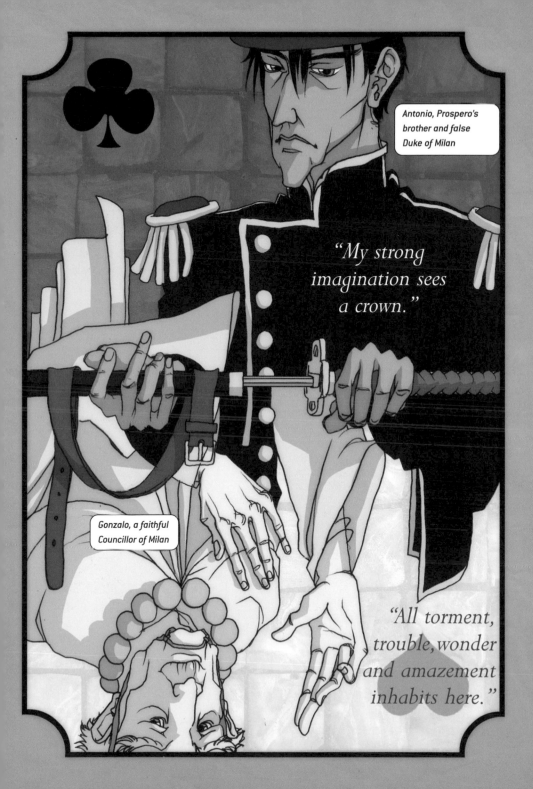

Prospero's Isle

The Rocky Steppe

The Abandoned
Factory

The Pine Woods

The Oil Fields

The Black
Beach

----- Ferdinand's Progress
----- Alonso, Antonio & Sebastian's Progress
----- Stephano's Progress
----- Trinculo's Progress
✕ Prospero's Cell

IF BY YOUR ART, MY DEAREST FATHER,

YOU HAVE PUT THE WILD WATERS IN THIS ROAR, ALLAY THEM.

A BRAVE VESSEL, DASHED ALL TO PIECES!

O! THE CRY DID KNOCK AGAINST MY HEART!

POOR SOULS, THEY PERISHED.

TELL YOUR PITEOUS HEART THERE'S NO HARM DONE.

MY BROTHER, AND THY UNCLE, CALLED ANTONIO, TO HIM PUT THE MANAGE OF MY STATE.

FOR THE LIBERAL ARTS BEING ALL MY STUDY, THE GOVERNMENT I CAST UPON MY BROTHER.

I, THUS NEGLECTING WORLDLY ENDS, ALL DEDICATED TO THE BETTERING OF MY MIND ...

IN MY FALSE BROTHER AWAKED AN EVIL NATURE. HE DID BELIEVE HE WAS INDEED DUKE.

DOST THOU HEAR?

YOUR TALE, SIR, WOULD CURE DEAFNESS.

27

THIS KING OF NAPLES, BEING AN ENEMY TO ME INVETERATE, HEARKENS MY BROTHER'S SUIT...

... WHICH WAS THAT HE SHOULD PRESENTLY EXTIRPATE ME AND MINE OUT OF THE DUKEDOM...

... AND CONFER FAIR MILAN, WITH ALL HONOURS, ON MY BROTHER.

WHEREON, A TREACHEROUS ARMY LEVIED, ONE MIDNIGHT DID ANTONIO OPEN THE GATES OF MILAN.

TAP TAP TAP TAP TAP TAP

AND, IN THE DEAD OF DARKNESS, THE MINISTERS FOR THE PURPOSE HURRIED THENCE ME AND THY CRYING SELF.

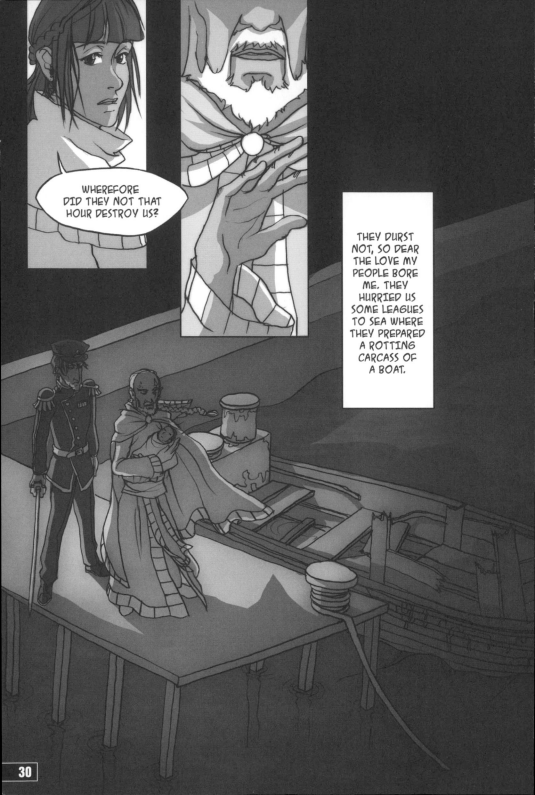

WHEREFORE DID THEY NOT THAT HOUR DESTROY US?

THEY DURST NOT, SO DEAR THE LOVE MY PEOPLE BORE ME. THEY HURRIED US SOME LEAGUES TO SEA WHERE THEY PREPARED A ROTTING CARCASS OF A BOAT.

THE VERY RATS INSTINCTIVELY HAVE QUIT IT.

THERE THEY HOIST US TO CRY TO THE SEA THAT ROARED TO US.

ALACK! WHAT TROUBLE WAS I THEN TO YOU.

O, A CHERUBIN THOU WAST THAT DID PRESERVE ME!

I BOARDED THE KING'S SHIP...

I FLAMED AMAZEMENT —

ON THE TOPMAST,

THE YARDS, AND BOWSPRIT...

JOVE'S LIGHTNINGS,
DREADFUL THUNDER CLAPS,

FIRE AND CRACKS OF
SULPHUROUS ROARING...

THE KING'S SON, FERDINAND,
WAS THE FIRST MAN THAT LEAPED.

HELL IS EMPTY,
AND ALL THE
DEVILS ARE
HERE.

THE KING'S SON
HAVE I LANDED
BY HIMSELF,

SITTING,
HIS ARMS IN
THIS SAD
KNOT.

THE REST OF THE FLEET, WHICH I DISPERSED,
THEY HAVE ALL MET AGAIN...

... AND ARE BOUND SADLY HOME FOR NAPLES...

... SUPPOSING THEY SAW THE KING'S SHIP WRECKED...

... AND HIS GREAT PERSON PERISH.

REFUSING HER GRAND BEHESTS, SHE DID CONFINE THEE INTO A CLOVEN PINE, WITHIN WHICH RIFT IMPRISONED, THOU DIDST PAINFULLY REMAIN A DOZEN YEARS.

SHE DIED AND LEFT THEE THERE, WHERE THOU DIDST VENT THY GROANS AS FAST AS MILL-WHEELS STRIKE.

SHE DID LITTER
HERE A FRECKLED
WHELP HAG-BORN
...
NOT HONOURED
WITH A HUMAN
SHAPE.

YES,
CALIBAN
HER SON.

HE, THAT
CALIBAN,
WHOM NOW
I KEEP IN
SERVICE.

THY GROANS
DID MAKE
WOLVES HOWL
AND PENETRATE
THE BREASTS
OF BEARS.

IT WAS A TORMENT WHICH SYCORAX COULD NOT AGAIN UNDO.

IT WAS MINE ART, WHEN I ARRIVED, THAT MADE GAPE THE PINE AND LET THEE OUT.

THE AIR BREATHES UPON US HERE MOST SWEETLY.

AS IF IT HAD LUNGS, AND ROTTEN ONES.

HERE IS EVERYTHING ADVANTAGEOUS TO LIFE.

TRUE, SAVE MEANS TO LIVE.

OF THAT THERE'S NONE OR LITTLE.

SIR, YOU MAY THANK YOURSELF FOR THIS GREAT LOSS, THAT WOULD NOT BLESS OUR EUROPE WITH YOUR DAUGHTER, BUT RATHER LOSE HER TO AN AFRICAN.

WE HAVE LOST YOUR SON, I FEAR, FOR EVER.

THE FAULT'S YOUR OWN.

MY LORD SEBASTIAN, YOU RUB THE SORE WHEN YOU SHOULD BRING THE PLASTER.

NO OCCUPATION,
ALL MEN IDLE, ALL.
AND WOMEN TOO, BUT
INNOCENT AND PURE.
NO SOVEREIGNTY.

YET HE WOULD
BE KING ON IT.

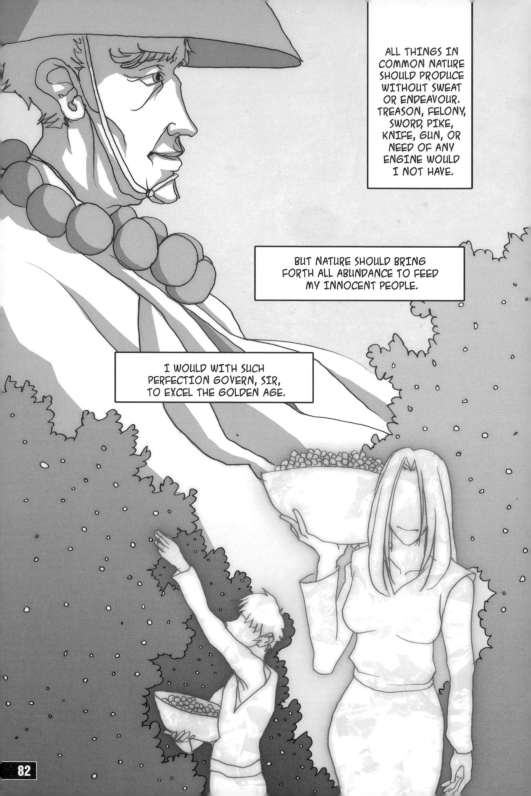

ALL THINGS IN COMMON NATURE SHOULD PRODUCE WITHOUT SWEAT OR ENDEAVOUR. TREASON, FELONY, SWORD, PIKE, KNIFE, GUN, OR NEED OF ANY ENGINE WOULD I NOT HAVE.

BUT NATURE SHOULD BRING FORTH ALL ABUNDANCE TO FEED MY INNOCENT PEOPLE.

I WOULD WITH SUCH PERFECTION GOVERN, SIR, TO EXCEL THE GOLDEN AGE.

WILL YOU GRANT WITH ME THAT FERDINAND IS DROWNED?

HE'S GONE.

THEN TELL ME, WHO'S THE NEXT HEIR OF NAPLES?

CLARIBEL.

SHE THAT IS QUEEN OF TUNIS, SHE THAT FROM NAPLES CAN HAVE NO NOTE.

MY MASTER THROUGH HIS ART FORESEES THE DANGER THAT YOU, HIS FRIEND, ARE IN...

WHILE YOU HERE DO SNORING LIE, OPEN-EYED CONSPIRACY HIS TIME DOTH TAKE...

SHAKE OFF SLUMBER AND BEWARE: AWAKE! AWAKE!

THIS IS NO FISH, BUT AN ISLANDER, THAT HATH LATELY SUFFERED BY A THUNDERBOLT.
MY BEST WAY IS TO CREEP UNDER HIS GABERDINE. THERE IS NO OTHER SHELTER HEREABOUT.
MISERY ACQUAINTS A MAN WITH STRANGE BEDFELLOWS.

"I SHALL NO MORE TO SEA, TO SEA, HERE SHALL I DIE ASHORE!"

THIS IS A VERY SCURVY TUNE TO SING AT A MAN'S FUNERAL.

WELL, HERE'S MY COMFORT.

DO NOT TORMENT ME! O!

107

THIS MY MEAN TASK WOULD BE HEAVY TO ME BUT THE MISTRESS WHICH I SERVE MAKES MY LABOURS PLEASURES.

MY SWEET MISTRESS WEEPS WHEN SHE SEES ME WORK.

THESE SWEET THOUGHTS DO REFRESH MY LABOURS.

ALAS! NOW PRAY YOU, WORK NOT SO HARD.

MY FATHER IS HARD AT STUDY. REST YOURSELF. HE'S SAFE FOR THESE THREE HOURS.

THE SUN WILL SET BEFORE I SHALL DISCHARGE WHAT I MUST STRIVE TO DO.

IF YOU'LL SIT DOWN, I'LL BEAR YOUR LOGS THE WHILE.

I AM IN MY CONDITION A PRINCE, MIRANDA.

HEAR MY SOUL SPEAK: THE VERY INSTANT THAT I SAW YOU DID MY HEART FLY TO YOUR SERVICE, THERE RESIDES TO MAKE ME SLAVE TO IT, AND FOR YOUR SAKE AM I THIS PATIENT LOG-MAN.

DO YOU LOVE ME?

REMEMBER FIRST TO POSSESS HIS BOOKS, FOR WITHOUT THEM HE HATH NOT ONE SPIRIT TO COMMAND. THEY ALL DO HATE HIM AS ROOTEDLY AS I. BURN BUT HIS BOOKS...

MOST DEEPLY TO CONSIDER IS THE BEAUTY OF HIS DAUGHTER. HE HIMSELF CALLS HER A NONPAREIL.

IS IT SO BRAVE A LASS?

I AM RIGHT GLAD THAT HE'S SO OUT OF HOPE.

DO NOT FORGO THE PURPOSE THAT YOU RESOLVED TO EFFECT.

THE NEXT ADVANTAGE WILL WE TAKE THOROUGHLY.

LET IT BE TONIGHT, FOR, NOW THEY ARE OPPRESSED WITH TRAVEL, THEY CANNOT USE SUCH VIGILANCE AS WHEN THEY ARE FRESH.

I SAY TONIGHT: NO MORE.

FOR WHICH FOUL DEED LINGERING
PERDITION — WORSE THAN ANY DEATH CAN BE AT ONCE — SHALL
STEP BY STEP ATTEND YOU AND YOUR WAYS HERE, IN THIS MOST
DESOLATE ISLE.

BRAVELY THE FIGURE OF THIS HARPY HAST THOU PERFORMED, MY ARIEL.

MY HIGH CHARMS WORK, AND THESE MINE ENEMIES ARE ALL KNIT UP.

I LEAVE THEM, WHILE I VISIT YOUNG FERDINAND AND HIS AND MINE LOVED DARLING.

145

I HAD FORGOT THAT FOUL CONSPIRACY OF THE BEAST CALIBAN AND HIS CONFEDERATES AGAINST MY LIFE.

THE MINUTE OF THEIR PLOT IS ALMOST COME.

YOUR FATHER'S IN SOME PASSION.

NEVER SAW I HIM SO DISTEMPERED.

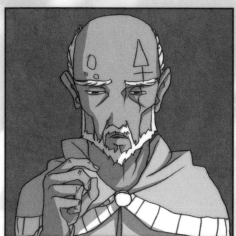

BE CHEERFUL, SIR, OUR REVELS NOW ARE ENDED.

THESE OUR ACTORS WERE ALL SPIRITS AND ARE MELTED INTO AIR. AND LIKE THE BASELESS FABRIC OF THIS VISION...

SIR,
I AM
VEXED.

RETIRE INTO
MY CELL.
I'LL WALK TO STILL
MY BEATING MIND.

WE
WISH
YOUR
PEACE.

WE NOW ARE NEAR HIS CELL.

MONSTER, I DO SMELL ALL HORSE-PISS.

DO YOU HEAR, MONSTER? IF I SHOULD TAKE A DISPLEASURE AGAINST YOU...

GOOD MY LORD, BE PATIENT FOR THE PRIZE I'LL BRING THEE TO.

BE QUIET, MONSTER.

MONSTER, COME, AWAY WITH THE REST.

WE SHALL LOSE OUR TIME AND ALL BE TURNED TO BARNACLES OR TO APES...

MONSTER, HELP TO BEAR THIS AWAY, OR I'LL TURN YOU OUT OF MY KINGDOM.

THE KING,
HIS BROTHER AND
YOURS ABIDE ALL
THREE DISTRACTED,
AND THE REMAINDER
MOURNING OVER
THEM, BRIMFUL OF
SORROW AND
DISMAY.

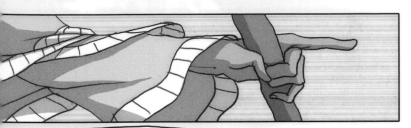

GO RELEASE THEM, ARIEL.
MY CHARMS I'LL BREAK,
THEIR SENSES I'LL RESTORE,
AND THEY SHALL BE THEMSELVES.

I'LL FETCH
THEM, SIR.

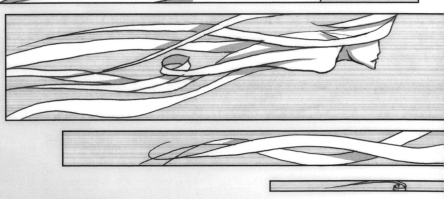

I HAVE BEDIMMED THE NOONTIDE SUN, CALLED FORTH THE MUTINOUS WINDS...

AND 'TWIXT THE GREEN SEA AND THE AZURED VAULT SET ROARING WAR. TO THE DREAD RATTLING THUNDER HAVE I GIVEN FIRE.

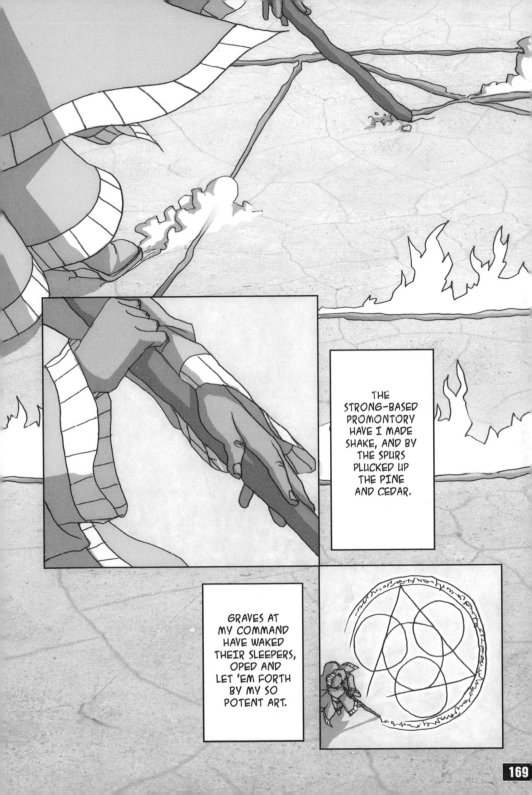

THE STRONG-BASED PROMONTORY HAVE I MADE SHAKE, AND BY THE SPURS PLUCKED UP THE PINE AND CEDAR.

GRAVES AT MY COMMAND HAVE WAKED THEIR SLEEPERS, OPED AND LET 'EM FORTH BY MY SO POTENT ART.

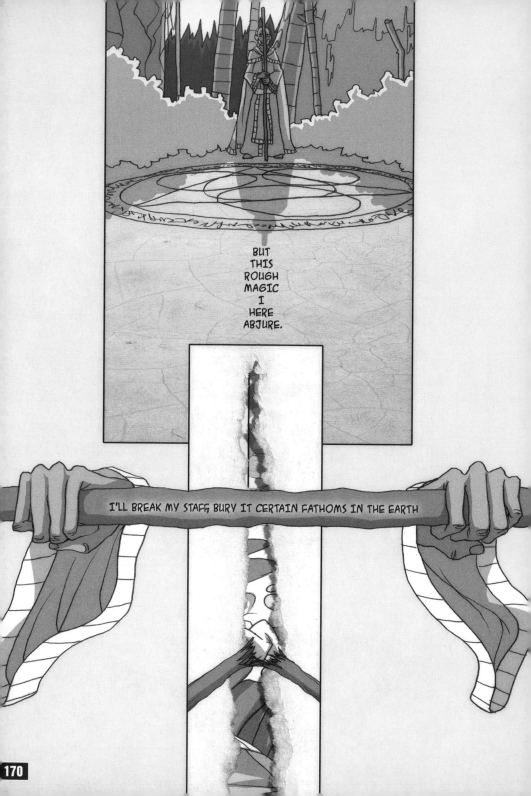

BUT
THIS
ROUGH
MAGIC
I
HERE
ABJURE.

I'LL BREAK MY STAFF BURY IT CERTAIN FATHOMS IN THE EARTH

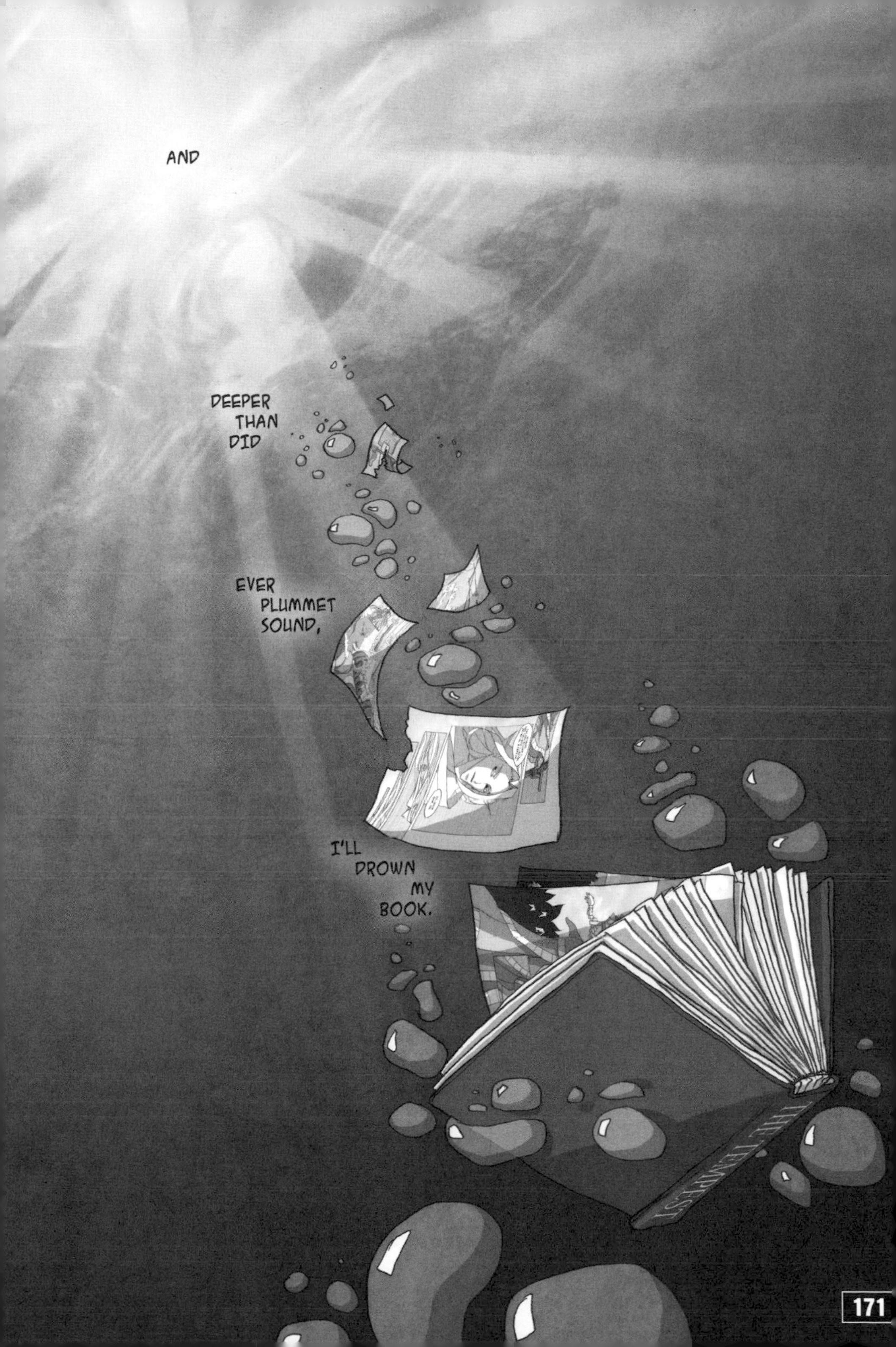

AND

DEEPER
THAN DID

EVER
PLUMMET
SOUND,

I'LL
DROWN
MY
BOOK.

THY BROTHER WAS A FURTHERER IN THE ACT. THOU ART PINCHED FOR IT NOW, SEBASTIAN.

YOU, BROTHER MINE, THAT ENTERTAINED AMBITION, EXPELLED REMORSE AND NATURE, WHO WITH SEBASTIAN WOULD HERE HAVE KILLED YOUR KING...

I DO FORGIVE THEE, UNNATURAL THOUGH THOU ART!

NOT ONE OF THEM THAT LOOKS ON ME WOULD KNOW ME.
ARIEL, FETCH ME THE HAT AND RAPIER IN MY CELL. I WILL MYSELF PRESENT AS I WAS SOMETIME MILAN.

WHERE THE BEE SUCKS, THERE SUCK I,
IN A COWSLIP'S BELL I LIE,
THERE I COUCH WHEN OWLS DO CRY.

ON THE BAT'S BACK I DO FLY.
MERRILY, MERRILY SHALL I LIVE NOW,
UNDER THE BLOSSOM THAT HANGS ON THE BOUGH.

ALL TORMENT, TROUBLE, WONDER AND AMAZEMENT INHABITS HERE.

SOME HEAVENLY POWER GUIDE US OUT OF THIS FEARFUL COUNTRY!

BEHOLD, SIR KING, THE WRONGED DUKE OF MILAN, PROSPERO.

TO THEE AND THY COMPANY I BID A HEARTY WELCOME.

FIRST, NOBLE FRIEND, LET ME EMBRACE THINE AGE, WHOSE HONOUR CANNOT BE MEASURED OR CONFINED.

.....

WHETHER THIS BE, OR NOT BE, I'LL NOT SWEAR.

YOU DO YET TASTE SOME SUBTLETIES OF THE ISLE THAT WILL NOT LET YOU BELIEVE THINGS CERTAIN.

IF THOU BE'ST PROSPERO, GIVE US PARTICULARS OF THY PRESERVATION.

HOW THOU HAST MET US HERE WHO THREE HOURS SINCE WERE WRECKED UPON THIS SHORE...

... WHERE I HAVE LOST MY DEAR SON FERDINAND.

I AM WOE FOR IT, SIR, FOR I HAVE LOST MY DAUGHTER.

185

189

O LOOK, SIR!

I PROPHESIED THIS FELLOW COULD NOT DROWN.

NOW, HAST THOU NO MOUTH BY LAND? WHAT IS THE NEWS?

THE BEST NEWS IS THAT WE HAVE SAFELY FOUND OUR KING AND COMPANY.

OUR SHIP IS TIGHT AND BRAVELY RIGGED AS WHEN WE FIRST PUT OUT TO SEA.

SIR, ALL THIS SERVICE HAVE I DONE SINCE I WENT.

MY TRICKSY SPIRIT!

THESE ARE NOT NATURAL EVENTS; THEY STRENGTHEN FROM STRANGE TO STRANGER.

STRAIGHTWAY, AT LIBERTY, WE FRESHLY BEHELD OUR ROYAL SHIP...

...OUR MASTER CAPERING TO EYE HER.

ON A TRICE, SO PLEASE YOU, EVEN IN A DREAM, WERE WE DIVIDED AND BROUGHT HITHER.

WAS IT WELL DONE?

BRAVELY, MY DILIGENCE! THOU SHALT BE FREE.

THIS MISSHAPEN KNAVE - HIS MOTHER WAS A WITCH THAT COULD CONTROL THE MOON. THESE THREE HAVE ROBBED ME AND PLOTTED TO TAKE MY LIFE.

I SHALL BE PINCHED TO DEATH.

IS NOT THIS STEPHANO, MY DRUNKEN BUTLER?

HE IS DRUNK NOW. WHERE HAD HE WINE?

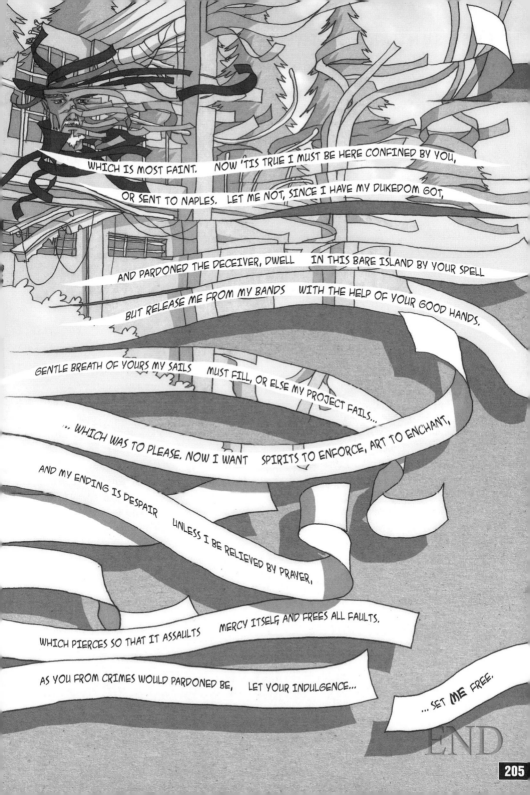

WHICH IS MOST FAINT.   NOW 'TIS TRUE I MUST BE HERE CONFINED BY YOU,

OR SENT TO NAPLES.   LET ME NOT, SINCE I HAVE MY DUKEDOM GOT,

AND PARDONED THE DECEIVER, DWELL   IN THIS BARE ISLAND BY YOUR SPELL

BUT RELEASE ME FROM MY BANDS   WITH THE HELP OF YOUR GOOD HANDS.

GENTLE BREATH OF YOURS MY SAILS   MUST FILL, OR ELSE MY PROJECT FAILS...

... WHICH WAS TO PLEASE. NOW I WANT   SPIRITS TO ENFORCE, ART TO ENCHANT,

AND MY ENDING IS DESPAIR   UNLESS I BE RELIEVED BY PRAYER,

WHICH PIERCES SO THAT IT ASSAULTS   MERCY ITSELF AND FREES ALL FAULTS.

AS YOU FROM CRIMES WOULD PARDONED BE,   LET YOUR INDULGENCE...

... SET ME FREE.

END

PLOT SUMMARY OF THE TEMPEST

This is the story of Prospero, the rightful Duke of Milan, who has been deposed by his treacherous brother Antonio. He conspired with Alonso, the King of Naples, to cast Prospero and his infant daughter Miranda adrift at sea. Both are presumed dead. In fact, however, Alonso's virtuous adviser Gonzalo had stocked their boat with supplies, enabling them to survive until washed ashore on a distant unknown island, where they have now been marooned for twelve years.

A powerful magician, and now lord of the island, Prospero is served by two native inhabitants: the spirit Ariel and the beast Caliban. Prospero has freed Ariel from the curse of endless imprisonment imposed by the witch Sycorax, now dead. Caliban is Sycorax's own grudging and malignant son.

With Ariel's help, Prospero now seizes the chance for revenge, conjuring up a great storm to wreck a ship, carrying his enemies, on to the shores of his island. On the ship are King Alonso, his son Ferdinand and brother Sebastian. Among the others aboard are kindly Gonzalo, Prospero's own brother Antonio, as well as other noblemen and servants. All of them are travelling back to Naples from the wedding in Africa of Alonso's daughter Claribel. Ariel puts the crew to sleep, leaving the castaways safely stranded – but at the mercy of Prospero's plans, which unfold over the next few hours.

The villainous Antonio now seeks to usurp the throne of Naples by persuading Sebastian to murder his brother, King Alonso – now distraught at what he believes to be the drowning of his son Ferdinand. Elsewhere, Alonso's servants, the drunken butler Stephano and the foolish Trinculo, encounter Caliban, who similarly persuades them to assassinate Prospero and take command of his island. Both these conspiracies, however, are closely monitored by Prospero, and each is frustrated by Ariel's enchantments, which lead them all astray.

Meanwhile, Ferdinand has been captured, alive and well, by Prospero, who pretends to enslave him – though his true aim is to test Ferdinand's character in the hope of supplying a worthy partner for his precious daughter Miranda. Prospero's plan works – the couple immediately fall in love – but how severely should he now punish those who have denied him his dukedom? In the end, love and forgiveness triumph over any wish for revenge, and all are reconciled as if awoken from a bad dream. Prospero will return to Milan, once more as its Duke, renounce magic, and at last set Ariel free in payment for his services. The island is Caliban's once more.

A BRIEF LIFE OF WILLIAM SHAKESPEARE

Shakespeare's birthday is traditionally said to be the 23rd of April — St George's Day, patron saint of England. A good start for England's greatest writer. But that date and even his name are uncertain. He signed his own name in different ways. "Shakespeare" is now the accepted one out of dozens of different versions.

He was born at Stratford-upon-Avon in 1564, and baptized on 26th April. His mother, Mary Arden, was the daughter of a prosperous farmer. His father, John Shakespeare, a glove-maker, was a respected civic figure — and probably also a Catholic. In 1570, just as Will began school, his father was accused of illegal dealings. The family fell into debt and disrepute.

Will attended a local school for eight years. He did not go to university. The next ten years are a blank filled by suppositions. Was he briefly a Latin teacher, a soldier, a sea-faring explorer? Was he prosecuted and whipped for poaching deer?

We do know that in 1582 he married Anne Hathaway, eight years his senior, and three months pregnant. Two more children — twins — were born three years later but, by around 1590, Will had left Stratford to pursue a theatre career in London. Shakespeare's apprenticeship began as an actor and "pen for hire".

He learned his craft the hard way. He soon won fame as a playwright with often-staged popular hits.

He and his colleagues formed a stage company, the Lord Chamberlain's Men, which built the famous Globe Theatre. It opened in 1599 but was destroyed by fire in 1613 during a performance of *Henry VIII* which used gunpowder special effects. It was rebuilt in brick the following year.

Shakespeare was a financially successful writer who invested his money wisely in property. In 1597, he bought an enormous house in Stratford, and in 1608 became a shareholder in London's Blackfriars Theatre. He also redeemed the family's honour by acquiring a personal coat of arms.

Shakespeare wrote over 40 works, including poems, "lost" plays and collaborations, in a career spanning nearly 25 years. He retired to Stratford in 1613, where he died on 23rd April 1616, aged 52, apparently of a fever after a "merry meeting" of drinks with friends. Shakespeare did in fact die on St George's Day! He was buried "full 17 foot deep" in Holy Trinity Church, Stratford, and left an epitaph cursing anyone who dared disturb his bones.

There have been preposterous theories disputing Shakespeare's authorship. Some claim that Sir Francis Bacon (1561–1626), philosopher and Lord Chancellor, was the real author of Shakespeare's plays. Others propose Edward de Vere, Earl of Oxford (1550–1604), or, even more weirdly, Queen Elizabeth I. The implication is that the "real" Shakespeare had to be a university graduate or an aristocrat. Nothing less would do for the world's greatest writer.

Shakespeare is mysteriously hidden behind his work. His life will not tell us what inspired his genius.

MANGA SHAKESPEARE ™

EDITORIAL

Richard Appignanesi: Series Editor

Richard Appignanesi was a founder and co-director of the Writers & Readers Publishing Cooperative and Icon Books where he originated the internationally acclaimed *Introducing* series. His own best-selling titles written for the series include *Freud*, *Postmodernism* and *Existentialism*. He is also the author of the fiction trilogy *Italia Perversa* and the novel *Yukio Mishima's Report to the Emperor*. He is currently associate editor of the art and culture journal *Third Text* and reviews editor of the journal *Futures*. His latest book *What do Existentialists Believe?* was released in 2006.

Nick de Somogyi: Textual Consultant

Nick de Somogyi works as a freelance writer and researcher, as a genealogist at the College of Arms, and as a contributing editor to *New Theatre Quarterly*. He is the founding editor of the Globe Quartos series, and was the visiting curator at Shakespeare's Globe, 2003–6. His publications include *Shakespeare's Theatre of War* (1998), *Jokermen and Thieves: Bob Dylan and the Ballad Tradition* (1986), and, as editor, *The Little Book of War Poems* (1999), and (from 2001) the *Shakespeare Folios* series for Nick Hern Books. His other work has included contributions to the Open University (1995) and Carlton Television (2000), BBC Radio 3 and Radio 4, and the National Portrait Gallery (2006).

ARTIST

Paul Duffield

Paul Duffield is an illustrator and animator who takes influence from a fusion of manga and European comics. After graduating with a BA in animation at Kingston, he went on to win both Tokyopop's Rising Stars of Manga, and the International Manga and Anime Festival grand prizes. His current projects include a collaboration with Kate Brown, artist for *A Midsummer Night's Dream*, a short story in *Best New Manga 2* and artwork for Warren Ellis on the webcomic *FreakAngels*.

PUBLISHER

SelfMadeHero publishes manga and graphic novels. It launched its first titles in the Manga Shakespeare series with *Hamlet* and *Romeo and Juliet*. Other titles already published include: *Richard III* and *A Midsummer Night's Dream*, with more to follow.

HAMLET

ROMEO AND JULIET

RICHARD III

A MIDSUMMER NIGHT'S DREAM

SELF MADE HERO

www.selfmadehero.com